Popcorn

Lovers

Recipe Book

Table of Contents

Introduction vi

Sweet Popcorn Recipes 1

   Caramel Apple Popcorn 2

   Peanut Butter Marshmallow Popcorn 3

   Orange Creamsicle Popcorn 4

   Lemon Brown Butter Popcorn 5

   French Onion Dip Popcorn 6

   Salt and Vinegar Popcorn 7

   Margarita Popcorn 8

   Blue Cheese and Almond Popcorn 9

   Party Cake Popcorn 9

   Maple Syrup Popcorn 10

   St. Patrick's Day Popcorn 11

   Jolly Rancher Popcorn Balls 12

   Sweet Cherry Popcorn 13

   Cherry Chocolate Popcorn 14

   Cookies and Cream Popcorn 14

   Cinnamon Buns Popcorn 16

   Marshmallow Popcorn 17

   Pecan Pie Popcorn 18

   Candy Corn Popcorn 19

   Cinnamon Apple Popcorn 20

   S'mores Popcorn 21

   Chocolate Caramel-Nut Popcorn 22

   Caramel Popcorn Bacon Mix 23

   Chocolate Popcorn 24

   Caramel Popcorn 25

   Peanut Butter Popcorn 26

   Peanut Butter and Banana Popcorn 27

   Tropical Popcorn 28

   Strawberry Popcorn 29

   Granola Yogurt Popcorn 30

Cinnamon Sugar Popcorn 31

Maple Pecan Popcorn 32

Marshmallow Popcorn 33

Rocky Road Popcorn 34

Cookies and Cream Popcorn...35

Peppermint Popcorn 36

Rum Carmel Popcorn 37

Kahlua and Espresso Bean Caramel Corn 38

Biscoff Popcorn...39

Cranberry Popcorn Snack Mix 40

White Chocolate Brown Sugar Popcorn.......................................41

Brownie Cookie Dough Popcorn...42

Chocolate Caramel Popcorn..43

Butter Pecan Cake Kettle Corn Popcorn 44

Spiced Chocolate Popcorn..45

White Chocolate Lemon Popcorn 45

Chocolate Crispies Popcorn...46

Peanut Butter and Jelly Popcorn 47

Bourbon Toffee Popcorn 48

Chocolate Caramel Popcorn..49

Pumpkin Pie Spice Popcorn 50

Chocolate Chip Cookie Popcorn...50

Toasted Coconut Popcorn...51

Kettle Corn Mix Popcorn...52

Savoury Popcorn Recipes 53

Cheesy Popcorn 54

Bacon Popcorn 55

Coconut Curry Popcorn 55

Ketchup Popcorn...56

Pizza Popcorn 57

Taco Popcorn...58

Sour Cream and Onion Popcorn 59

Doritos Popcorn 60

Popcorn Nachos 60

Lemon Butter Popcorn 61

Ranch Popcorn 61

Garlic Herb Popcorn 62

Parmesan Rosemary Popcorn 62

Frito Popcorn 63

Truffle Popcorn 63

Veggie Delight Popcorn 64

Crunchy Ramen Popcorn 64

Three-Cheese Popcorn 65

Gourmet Mushroom Cheese Popcorn 65

Everything Bagel Popcorn 66

Bacon Chive Popcorn 66

Movie Theater Popcorn 67

Vanilla Popcorn 68

Dill Pickle Popcorn 69

Spicy Popcorn Recipes 70

Wasabi Soy Sauce Popcorn 71

Mustard Pretzel Popcorn 71

Jamaican Jerk Popcorn 72

Za'atar Popcorn 73

Mole Popcorn 74

Cajun Popcorn 75

Barbecue Popcorn 76

Bacon Jalapeno Popcorn 77

Spicy Pork Rind Popcorn 78

Tex Mex Popcorn 79

Szechuan Popcorn 80

Sriracha Lime Popcorn 80

Chipotle Popcorn 82

Spicy Sesame Popcorn 82

Sushi Popcorn 83

Buffalo Wings Popcorn 84

Chili Popcorn 85

Jalapeno Popcorn 86

Curry Popcorn 86

Thai Curry Popcorn 87

Red Hots Popcorn 88

Maryland Crab Cake Popcorn 89

About the Author 91

Other books by Laura Sommers 92

Introduction

Popcorn is as American as apple pie! It was first introduced by the Iroquois tribe of Native Americans in New Mexico. Being a cheap and low calorie snack food, it gained in popularity during the Great Depression. It further gained in popularity by being eaten in movie theaters during the Golden Era of film and became the main ingredient of boxed snack foods such as Cracker Jacks and Fiddle Faddle.

Today it is widely popular amongst financially strapped college students looking for a quick and easy snack. It is also great during holidays as a party food. During today's tough economic times it makes a great inexpensive snack food for families.

I have put together this collection of popcorn recipes to help add pizazz to one of American's favorite snack foods. They are separated into three categories: Sweet, Spicy and Savory. Whenever possible the recipes use microwave popcorn as the main ingredient, however, they can be adapted for using popcorn kernels. The one caveat is air popped popcorn, which may melt if some of the more heavier and sugary toppings are poured on top. There are also a few instances when it is necessary to use kernels instead of microwave popcorn. I hope that you enjoy!

Sweet Popcorn Recipes

Caramel Apple Popcorn

Ingredients:

3 bags microwave popcorn
2 (2.5 oz.) bags of apple chips
1 cup light brown sugar
1 cup light corn syrup
½ cup butter
1 tsp salt
1 (14 oz.) can of sweetened condensed milk

Directions:

1. Preheat oven to 250 degrees.
2. Pop popcorn in microwave according to package directions.
3. Pick out any un-popped kernels.
4. In a saucepan over medium heat, combine brown sugar, butter, corn syrup and salt.
5. Heat until melted and begins to boil.
6. Once boiling, add the condensed milk and stir continuously for 5 minutes, to prevent burning.
7. Remove from heat and pour directly over popcorn and apples, stirring until coated evenly.
8. Place in preheated oven and bake for 45-50 minutes, stirring every 10 minutes.
9. Remove from oven, break into pieces and allow to cool.
10. Serve and enjoy!

Peanut Butter Marshmallow Popcorn

Ingredients:

2 bags microwave popcorn
1/2 cup margarine
3/4 cup brown sugar
1/4 cup peanut butter
20 large marshmallows

Directions:

1. Pop popcorn in microwave according to package directions.
2. Pick out any un-popped kernels.
3. Pour popcorn into a large bowl.
4. In a bowl, combine the margarine, brown sugar, and marshmallows.
5. Cook at short 1 minute intervals in the microwave, stirring each time, until the mixture is melted.
6. Stir in the peanut butter until well blended.
7. Pour the melted mixture over the popcorn, and stir quickly to coat the corn before it cools.
8. Serve and enjoy!

Orange Creamsicle Popcorn

Ingredients:

2 pkgs. microwave popcorn
16 oz. vanilla candy coating
Scrapings of vanilla bean
Orange zest, from one large orange

Directions:

1. Pop popcorn in microwave according to package directions.
2. Pick out any unpopped kernels.
3. Melt the candy coating according to direction packages until it is completely smooth.
4. Stir in vanilla beans and orange zest until completely incorporated.
5. Pour melted candy coating mixture over the popcorn mixture.
6. Stir until everything is well coated.
7. Spread onto a large sheet pan for candy coating to harden.
8. Break in to pieces.
9. Serve and enjoy!

Lemon Brown Butter Popcorn

Ingredients:

2 pkgs. microwave popcorn
6 tbsps. butter
1 1/2 tsps. grated lemon zest
2 tsps. kosher salt

Directions:

1. Pop popcorn in microwave according to package directions.
2. Cook butter in a skillet over medium heat until browned, about 7 minutes.
3. Remove from the heat and stir in grated lemon zest.
4. drizzle over hot popcorn.
5. Toss with kosher salt.
6. Serve and enjoy!

French Onion Dip Popcorn

Ingredients:

6 tbsps. butter
1 (1 oz.) packet onion soup mix
2 pkgs. microwave popcorn
1 (6 oz.) package French-fried onions

Directions:

1. Pop popcorn in microwave according to package directions.
2. Melt butter with onion soup mix.
3. Toss with hot popcorn and French-fried onions.
4. Serve and enjoy!

Salt and Vinegar Popcorn

Ingredients:

2 pkgs. microwave popcorn
1/4 cup malt vinegar
2 tsps. kosher salt

Directions:

1. Pop popcorn in microwave according to directions.
2. Combine vinegar and kosher salt in a small spray bottle.
3. Shake to dissolve the salt.
4. Spray popcorn.
5. Serve and enjoy!

Margarita Popcorn

Ingredients:

2 pkgs. microwave popcorn
6 tbsps. butter
2 tbsps. lime juice
2 tbsps. tequila
2 tsps. sugar
2 tsps. kosher salt
1 1/2 tsps. grated lime zest
4 cups lime-flavored tortilla chips, lightly crushed

Directions:

1. Pop popcorn in microwave according to package directions.
2. Melt butter with lime juice, tequila, sugar, kosher salt and lime zest in a skillet over medium heat.
3. Drizzle over popcorn.
4. Toss with lime-flavored tortilla chips.
5. Serve and enjoy!

Blue Cheese and Almond Popcorn

Ingredients:

2 pkgs. Microwave popcorn
4 tbsps. melted butter
1 cup sliced almonds, toasted
1 cup crumbled blue cheese
1 tsp. kosher salt

Directions:

1. Pop popcorn in microwave according to package directions.
2. Drizzle melted butter over popcorn.
3. Toss with crumbled blue cheese, toasted sliced almonds, and kosher salt.
4. Serve and enjoy!

Party Cake Popcorn

Ingredients:

1 bag microwave popcorn, lightly salted
6-7 ounces white candy melts
Multicolored nonpareils (The sprinkles that look like colored balls)

Directions:

1. Pop popcorn in microwave according to directions.
2. Pick out any un-popped kernels.
3. Melt the candy melts slowly by putting in a Pyrex cup and microwaving at 30 seconds at a time, stirring each time.
4. In a large bowl, gently mix the melted candy into the popped popcorn.
5. Add the sprinkles before melted candy hardens and gently mix together.
6. Serve and enjoy!

Maple Syrup Popcorn

Ingredients:
2 bags of plain microwave popcorn
1 cup real maple syrup

1 cup walnut pieces
Nonstick cooking spray

Directions:

1. Pop popcorn in microwave according to directions.
2. Spray a large bowl and spoon with nonstick cooking spray.
3. Pour popcorn into the bowl.
4. Pick out any un-popped kernels.
5. Heat maple syrup over medium heat until syrup reaches 236 degrees on a candy thermometer.
6. Add the nuts to the popcorn.
7. Add the syrup to the popcorn and nut mixture and mix with the spoon that you sprayed.
8. When mixture cools, break in to pieces.
9. Serve and enjoy!

St. Patrick's Day Popcorn

Ingredients:

2 bags microwave popcorn
1 cup miniature marshmallows
3/4 cup chocolate candies, divided
1-1/2 cups fudge mint cookies, chopped & divided
1-1/2 cups white chocolate chips
1 tsp. shortening
1/4 cup green candy melts
3 Tbsps. sprinkles

Directions:

1. Pop popcorn in microwave according to directions.
2. Pick out any un-popped kernels.
3. Combine popcorn, marshmallows, 1/2 cup chocolate candies, and 1 cup fudge mint cookies pieces in a large bowl.
4. Crush the extra 1/2 cup cookies into crumbs and set aside with the extra chocolate candies.
5. In a microwave safe bowl, combine the white chips and shortening.
6. Heat slowly, stirring every 30 seconds until melted.
7. Pour over popcorn mixture and toss until everything is coated.
8. Spread out on a wax paper lined cookie tray.
9. Sprinkle with the crushed cookies and the extra 1/4 cup chocolate candies.
10. Let set.
11. Heat the green candy melts in a microwave safe bowl.
12. Spoon into a plastic bag and cut the tip off one corner.
13. Drizzle over the popcorn and top with sprinkles.
14. Let set before eating.
15. Serve and enjoy!

Jolly Rancher Popcorn Balls

Ingredients:

3 bags microwave popcorn
1 cup corn syrup
1/2 cup sugar
1 package of Jolly Rancher gelatin

Directions:

1. Pop popcorn in microwave according to directions.
2. Pick out any un-popped kernels.
3. Pour popcorn in a large bowl.
4. Lay out a sheet of parchment paper to place the popcorn balls on.
5. Place a bowl of cold water next to the bowl of popcorn.
6. Mix the first all ingredients except for the popcorn in a sauce pan.
7. Bring this mixture to a boil and cook until the gelatin and sugar have dissolved.
8. Remove from heat as soon as the ingredients are melted and no longer (about 1 minute)
9. Pour over the popcorn.
10. Mix well.
11. Wet your hands in the cold water and then form the popcorn in to balls about 1 cup in size.
12. Repeatedly dip your hands in the cold water as needed to prevent the mixture from sticking to your hands as you work.
13. You can wrap the balls in wax paper or cling wrap.
14. Cling wrap sticks to the popcorn balls more but it is easier to wrap them.
15. Serve and enjoy!

Sweet Cherry Popcorn

Ingredients:

2 bags microwave popcorn
3/4 cup candied red cherries, cut up
1 cup chopped pecans
3/4 cup packed brown sugar
6 tbsp. butter
1/4 tsp.. baking soda
1/4 tsp. vanilla
3 tsp. light corn syrup

Directions:

1. Preheat oven to 300 degrees.
2. Pop popcorn in microwave according to directions.
3. Pick out any un-popped kernels.
4. Pour popcorn in an ungreased 13"x9"2-inch baking pan.
5. Add cherries, and pecans.
6. Mix brown sugar, butter and corn syrup in a saucepan over medium heat until it comes to a boil.
7. Cook over low heat for 5 minutes more.
8. Remove from heat.
9. Stir in baking soda and vanilla.
10. Pour mixture over popcorn and pecans and stir until all the popcorn is coated.
11. Bake for 15 minutes.
12. Stir, and bake an additional 5-10 minutes.
13. Remove from oven and place in large bowl to cool.
14. Serve and enjoy!

Cherry Chocolate Popcorn

Ingredients:

2 bags microwave popcorn
1 cup sugar
1/3 cup whole milk
1 tbsp. light corn syrup
1/2 tsp. cherry flavoring
4-5 drops pink food coloring
1/4 cup chocolate, melted
1/2 cup chocolate chunks
1/4 cup glacé cherries, diced

Directions:

1. Pop popcorn in microwave according to directions.
2. Pick out any un-popped kernels.
3. Add popcorn into a large mixing bowl to cool.
4. Lay wax paper on a cookie sheet, and spray lightly with cooking spray.
5. Combine sugar, milk, corn syrup, and salt in a saucepan.
6. Bring mixture to a boil over medium heat, stirring occasionally, and then reduce heat slightly so the mixture simmers.
7. Continue to cook for about 4-6 minutes until you've reached a soft ball stage or 235 degrees on a candy thermometer.
8. Remove from heat, and stir in cherry flavoring and food coloring.
9. Pour the candy over your popcorn, and toss to combine.
10. Spread the coated popcorn out on wax paper, separating it as much as possible.
11. Drizzle with melted chocolate.
12. Quickly sprinkle with chocolate chunks and glacé cherries.
13. Salt to taste.
14. Let the mixture set.
15. Break up into chunks.
16. Serve and enjoy!

Cookies and Cream Popcorn

Ingredients:

2 bags of microwave popcorn

Non-stick cooking spray
6 cups miniature marshmallows, divided
6 tbsps. butter, divided
4 cups crushed chocolate sandwich cookies, divided
1 cup premier white morsels, divided

Directions:

1. Pop popcorn in microwave according to directions.
2. Pick out any un-popped kernels.
3. Spray bowl with non-stick cooking spray.
4. Put one bag of popped corn in a bowl.
5. Place 3 cups marshmallows and 3 tbsps. butter in microwave-safe bowl.
6. Microwave on high for about 45 seconds or until marshmallows melt and mixture blends together smoothly when stirred.
7. Pour marshmallow mixture over popped corn in bowl.
8. Spray rubber spatula with cooking spray.
9. Toss with rubber spatula to coat.
10. Add 2 cups crushed cookies and stir to combine.
11. Add 1/2 cup morsels and stir to combine.
12. Spray wax paper with cooking spray.
13. Divide mixture and shape into 6 balls.
14. Place on waxed paper.
15. Repeat above steps with remaining popped corn, marshmallows, butter, crushed cookies and morsels.
16. Serve and enjoy!

Cinnamon Buns Popcorn

Ingredients:

3 bags of microwave popcorn
1/4 cup Sugar
1 1/2 tsps. cinnamon
1/4 cup butter, melted
1 tsp. Pure vanilla extract

Directions:

1. Pop popcorn in microwave according to directions.
2. Pick out any un-popped kernels.
3. Combine sugar and cinnamon in a small bowl.
4. Set aside.
5. Combine melted butter and vanilla.
6. Set aside.
7. In a large bowl toss hot popcorn with butter coating evenly.
8. Add the cinnamon sugar and toss again.
9. Serve and enjoy!

Marshmallow Popcorn

Ingredients:

2 bags of microwave popcorn
1/2 cup brown sugar
1/2 cup butter
10 marshmallows

Directions:

1. Pop popcorn in microwave according to directions.
2. Pick out any un-popped kernels.
3. In a medium bowl, microwave brown sugar and butter for 2 minutes.
4. Add the marshmallows.
5. Microwave until melted (about 1 minute).
6. Pour the mixture over popcorn and mix well.
7. Serve and enjoy!

Pecan Pie Popcorn

Ingredients:

2 bags of microwave popcorn
Nonstick cooking spray
1/2 cup broken pecans
2 tbsps. butter or margarine
1/3 cup light corn syrup
1/4 cup instant butterscotch or butter pecan pudding mix
3/4 tsp. vanilla

Directions:

Preheat oven to 300 degrees.
1. Pop popcorn in microwave according to directions.
2. Pick out any un-popped kernels.
3. Spray a 17x12x2-inch roasting pan with nonstick cooking spray.
4. Place the popped corn and pecans in the pan.
5. In a small saucepan melt the margarine or butter.
6. Remove saucepan from heat.
7. Stir in the corn syrup, pudding mix, and vanilla.
8. Pour syrup mixture over popcorn.
9. Gently toss the popcorn with the syrup mixture to coat.
10. Bake popcorn, uncovered for 16 minutes, stirring halfway through baking.
11. Remove the pan from the oven.
12. Turn mixture onto a large piece of foil.
13. Cool popcorn completely.
14. Break into large pieces.
15. Serve and enjoy!

Candy Corn Popcorn

Ingredients:

2 bags of plain microwave popcorn
1/2 cup sugar
Cooking spray
1 cup candy corn
1/2 cup salted roasted peanuts
4 cups mini marshmallows
4 tbsps. unsalted butter

Directions:

1. Pop popcorn in microwave according to directions.
2. Spray a large bowl with cooking spray and add the popcorn, candy corn and peanuts.
3. Combine the marshmallows and butter in a large pot over medium-high heat.
4. Cook, stirring, until melted and smooth, about 5 minutes.
5. Pour the melted marshmallow mixture over the popcorn mixture
6. Gently toss to coat.
7. Put on rubber gloves and coat your hands with cooking spray.
8. Shape the popcorn into 3-inch balls.
9. Let cool.
10. Serve and enjoy!

Cinnamon Apple Popcorn

Ingredients:

3 bags of plain microwave popcorn
2 cups chopped dried apples
2 cups pecan halves
4 tbsps. butter, melted
1 tsp. cinnamon
1/4 tsp. nutmeg
2 tbsps. brown sugar
1/4 tsp. vanilla extract

Directions:

1. Pop popcorn in microwave according to directions.
2. Pick out any un-popped kernels.
3. Preheat oven to 250 degrees.
4. Place apples in a large shallow baking pan.
5. Bake for 20 minutes.
6. Remove pan from oven and stir in popcorn and nuts.
7. In a small bowl combine the remaining ingredients.
8. Drizzle butter mixture over popcorn mixture, stirring well.
9. Bake for 30 minutes, stirring every 10 minutes.
10. Pour onto wax paper to cool.
11. Store in air tight container.
12. Serve and enjoy!

S'mores Popcorn

Ingredients:

3 bags of microwave popcorn
1 cup brown sugar, firmly packed
½ cup butter or ½ cup margarine
½ cup corn syrup
½ tsp. baking soda
1 (10 1/2 ounce) package mini marshmallows
2 cups Teddy Grahams honey graham snacks (not crumbs) or 2 cups crumbled graham crackers (not crumbs)
1 cup chocolate chips

Directions:

1. Pop popcorn in microwave according to directions.
2. Let cool.
3. Pick out any un-popped kernels.
4. Combine the brown sugar, butter and corn syrup in a medium saucepan.
5. Cook on high for 5 minutes.
6. Remove the pan from the heat and stir in the baking soda.
7. Thoroughly combine the popcorn and marshmallows in a large metal bowl. (plastic bowls will melt)
8. Drizzle the sugar mixture over the popcorn to coat it.
9. Gently stir in the graham crackers and chocolate chips until mixed evenly throughout.
10. Let cool enough to touch, then, using buttered plastic sandwich bags on your hands, form the mixture into golf-ball-size balls.
11. Store in airtight container.
    12. Serve and enjoy!

Chocolate Caramel-Nut Popcorn

Ingredients:

2 pkgs. microwave popcorn
1/2 cup butter
1 cup brown sugar
1 tsp. salt
1/4 cup corn syrup
1 tsp. vanilla extract
1/2 tsp. baking soda
1 cup chocolate chips
1 cup sliced almonds
1/2 cup shredded coconut

Directions:

1. Preheat oven to 250 degrees F (120 degrees C).
2. Pop popcorn according to directions.
3. Pour into a very large bowl, and set aside.
4. Melt butter in a saucepan over medium heat.
5. Stir in the brown sugar, salt, and corn syrup.
6. Bring mixture to a boil, then reduce heat and simmer for 5 minutes, stirring constantly.
7. Take the saucepan off of the heat, and carefully stir in the vanilla extract and baking soda.
8. Pour the caramel over the popcorn and stir well.
9. Add the chocolate chips and almonds, then stir until thoroughly mixed.
10. Pour this mixture into two large, deep baking pans and sprinkle with the shredded coconut.
11. Serve and enjoy!

Caramel Popcorn Bacon Mix

Ingredients:

2 pkgs. microwave popcorn
1 (12 oz.) package thick-cut bacon
1/2 cup real maple syrup
2 cups crispy rice cereal squares (such as Rice Chex)
2 cups crispy wheat cereal squares (such as Wheat Chex)
2 cups peanuts
2 cups pretzel sticks
1 cup butter
2 cups brown sugar
1/2 cup corn syrup 1 tsp. salt
1 tsp. vanilla extract
1/2 tsp. baking soda

Directions:

1. Pop popcorn in microwave according to directions.
2. Line a baking sheet with aluminum foil.
3. Arrange bacon slices close together and slightly overlapping onto the prepared baking sheet.
4. Drizzle bacon slices evenly with maple syrup.
5. Place the baking sheet in the cold oven; set temperature to 400 degrees F (200 degrees C).
6. Bake until bacon is crisp, about 20 minutes.
7. Transfer bacon slices to a paper towel-lined plate to cool. Crumble cooled bacon.
8. Reduce oven temperature to 250 degrees F (120 degrees C).
9. Line 2 baking sheets with aluminum foil.
10. Lightly mix popcorn, rice cereal, wheat cereal, peanuts, pretzels, and crumbled bacon together in a large bowl.
11. Transfer to the prepared baking sheets.
12. Melt butter in a saucepan over medium heat; mix brown sugar, corn syrup, and salt into the melted butter.
13. Cook, stirring constantly, until mixture begins to boil. Boil mixture, without stirring, for 4 minutes.
14. Place popcorn mixture in the preheated oven to warm.
15. Remove the butter mixture from heat and mix in vanilla extract and baking soda until caramel begins to foam.
16. Drizzle caramel in a thin stream over popcorn mixture, tossing to evenly coat.

17. Bake caramel corn in the oven, stirring every 15 minutes, until caramel coating is set, 1 hour.
18. Let caramel corn cool completely before breaking into pieces.
19. Serve and enjoy!

Chocolate Popcorn

Ingredients:

2 pkgs. microwave popcorn
1 cup peanuts (optional)
3/4 cup sugar
1/4 cup corn syrup
1/4 cup cocoa powder
1/2 cup butter
1 tsp. vanilla

Directions:

1. Pop popcorn in microwave according to directions.
2. Preheat oven to 250 degrees F (120 degrees C).
3. Oil a 10x15 inch baking pan with sides.
4. Place popcorn and peanuts into a large, metal bowl, and set aside.
5. Stir together the sugar, corn syrup, cocoa powder, and butter in a saucepan over medium-high heat until it comes to a boil.
6. Boil for 2 minutes.
7. Stir in the vanilla, then pour over the popcorn.
8. Stir until the popcorn is well coated.
9. Spread the popcorn into the prepared pan.
10. Bake in preheated oven for 30 minutes, stirring several times.
11. Remove from the oven, and allow to cool to room temperature.
12. Break into small clumps.
13. Serve and enjoy!

Caramel Popcorn

Ingredients:

3 pkgs. microwave popcorn
1 cup butter
2 cups brown sugar
1/2 cup corn syrup
1 tsp. salt
1/2 tsp. baking soda
1 tsp. vanilla extract

Directions:

1. Pop popcorn in microwave according to directions.
2. Preheat oven to 250 degrees F (95 degrees C).
3. Place popcorn in a very large bowl.
4. In a medium saucepan over medium heat, melt butter.
5. Stir in brown sugar, corn syrup and salt. Bring to a boil, stirring constantly.
6. Boil without stirring 4 minutes.
7. Remove from heat and stir in soda and vanilla.
8. Pour in a thin stream over popcorn, stirring to coat.
9. Place in two large shallow baking dishes.
10. Bake in preheated oven, stirring every 15 minutes, for 1 hour.
11. Remove from oven and let cool completely before breaking into pieces.
12. Serve and enjoy!

Peanut Butter Popcorn

Ingredients:

2 pkgs. microwave popcorn
1 cup honey
3/4 cup sugar
1 cup peanut butter
1 tsp. vanilla extract
1 tsp. kosher salt
16 cups hot popcorn
2 cups peanuts

Directions:

1. Pop popcorn in microwave according to package directions.
2. In a medium pan, heat honey and sugar over medium heat, stirring, until the sugar dissolves, about 5 minutes.
3. Stir in peanut butter, vanilla extract and kosher salt until smooth.
4. Toss together popcorn and peanuts in a large bowl.
5. Pour peanut butter mixture over popcorn and peanuts and toss again.
6. Spread on baking sheets and let cool.
7. Break apart.
8. Serve and enjoy!

Peanut Butter and Banana Popcorn

Ingredients:

2 pkgs. microwave popcorn
1 cup honey
3/4 cup sugar
1 cup peanut butter
1 tsp. vanilla extract
1 tsp. kosher salt
2 cups peanuts
1 cup dried banana chips, lightly crushed
1/2 cup chocolate chips

Directions:

1. Pop popcorn in microwave according to package directions.
2. In a medium pan, heat honey and sugar over medium heat, stirring, until the sugar dissolves, about 5 minutes.
3. Stir in peanut butter, vanilla extract and kosher salt until smooth.
4. Toss together popcorn, banana chips, chocolate chips and peanuts in a large bowl.
5. Pour peanut butter mixture over popcorn and peanuts and toss again.
6. Spread on baking sheets and let cool.
7. Break apart.
8. Serve and enjoy!

Tropical Popcorn

Ingredients:

2 pkgs. microwave popcorn
2 cups sweetened shredded coconut
1 1/2 cups dried pineapple, chopped
3 tbsps. confectioners' sugar
3 tbsps. melted butter
Salt to taste

Directions:

1. Pop popcorn in microwave according to package directions.
2. Preheat oven to 350 degrees F.
3. Spread coconut on a baking sheet and bake until golden, about 10 minutes.
4. Toss popcorn with coconut, dried pineapple, confectioners' sugar and melted butter.
5. Salt to taste.
6. Serve and enjoy!

Strawberry Popcorn

Ingredients:

2 pkgs. microwave popcorn
2 cups freeze-dried strawberries, divided
6 tbsps. confectioners' sugar
4 tbsps. melted butter
1 cup freeze-dried strawberries

Directions:

1. Pop popcorn in microwave according to package directions.
2. Pulse 1 cup of the freeze-dried strawberries with the confectioners' sugar in a food processor until powdery.
3. Drizzle melted butter over popcorn.
4. Sprinkle with the strawberry sugar.
5. Toss popcorn with remaining freeze-dried strawberries.
6. Serve and enjoy!

Granola Yogurt Popcorn

Ingredients:

2 pkgs. microwave popcorn
6 tbsps. butter
2 tbsps. brown sugar
2 tbsps. honey
4 cups granola
2 cups yogurt-covered raisins

Directions:

1. Pop popcorn in microwave according to package directions.
2. In a medium saucepan, melt butter with brown sugar and honey over medium heat, stirring, until the sugar dissolves, 3 minutes.
3. Drizzle over popcorn.
4. Toss with granola and yogurt-covered raisins.
5. Season with salt.
6. Serve and enjoy!

Cinnamon Sugar Popcorn

Ingredients:

2 pkgs. microwave popcorn
6 tbsps. melted butter
4 cups cinnamon cereal
1/3 cup sugar
2 tsps. cinnamon
1 tsp. kosher salt

Directions:

1. Pop popcorn in microwave according to package directions.
2. Drizzle melted butter over popcorn.
3. Toss popcorn together with cinnamon cereal, sugar, cinnamon and kosher salt.
4. Serve and enjoy!

Maple Pecan Popcorn

Ingredients:

2 pkgs. microwave popcorn
2 cups sugar
1 cup maple syrup
1/2 cup light corn syrup
3 cups pecans
3 tbsps. butter

Directions:

1. Pop popcorn in microwave according to package directions.
2. Heat sugar, maple syrup and corn syrup in a large pot until it reaches 260 degrees F on a candy thermometer, about 12 minutes.
3. Add pecans and cook 2 minutes.
4. Stir in butter until melted.
5. Pour over popcorn.
6. Toss to coat.
7. Spread on baking sheets and let cool.
8. Break apart.
9. Serve and enjoy!

Marshmallow Popcorn

Ingredients:

2 pkgs. microwave popcorn
8 cups mini marshmallows
6 tbsps. butter with
1/2 cup sugar
1/2 cup light corn syrup
4 cups cornflakes
Salt to taste

Directions:

1. Pop popcorn in microwave according to package directions.
2. Melt marshmallows and butter with sugar and light corn syrup in a large saucepan over medium heat, stirring.
3. Pour over popcorn.
4. Add cornflakes and mix well.
5. Season with salt.
6. Serve and enjoy!

Rocky Road Popcorn

Ingredients:

2 pkgs. microwave popcorn
5 tbsps. melted butter
2 tsps. vanilla extract
2 tsps. kosher salt
2 cups mini marshmallows
2 cups chocolate chips
2 cups toasted pecans

Directions:

1. Pop popcorn in microwave according to package directions.
2. Preheat oven to 350 degrees F.
3. Whisk melted butter with vanilla extract and kosher salt.
4. Drizzle over 16 cups hot popcorn.
5. Toss with 2 cups each mini marshmallows, chocolate chips and toasted pecans.
6. Spread on baking sheets and bake until the marshmallows and chocolate are slightly melted, about 2 minutes.
7. Serve and enjoy!

Cookies and Cream Popcorn

Ingredients:

2 pkgs. microwave popcorn
1/4 cup sweetened condensed milk
4 cups chocolate sandwich cookies (such as Oreos), lightly crushed

Directions:

1. Pop popcorn in microwave according to package directions.
2. Warm sweetened condensed milk in a saucepan over medium heat.
3. Drizzle over popcorn.
4. Toss with cookies.
5. Serve and enjoy!

Peppermint Popcorn

Ingredients:

2 pkgs. microwave popcorn
16 ounce package white chocolate candy melts
1/2 tsp. peppermint extract
10 regular-sized candy canes, unwrapped
1 cup chocolate chips

Directions:

1. Pop popcorn in microwave according to directions.
2. Place candy canes in a large zip-top bag and crush using a rolling-pin or meat tenderizer.
3. Pick out the unpoped kernels.
4. In a very large bowl or a foil roasting pan, add popped popcorn, crushed candy canes, and chocolate chips.
5. Melt candy melts according to package directions.
6. Stir in peppermint extract.
7. Pour melted candy melts over popcorn mixture and stir well so that everything is coated.
8. Spread on two large baking sheets until hardened.
9. Break apart.
10. Serve and enjoy!

Rum Carmel Popcorn

Ingredients:

2 pkgs. microwave popcorn
3 cups of granulated white sugar
1/4 cup dark rum
3 tbsps. unsalted butter
1 tbsp. pure vanilla extract
1.5 tsps. salt
1.5 tsps. baking soda

Directions:

1. Pop popcorn in microwave according to directions.
2. Place popped popcorn in a large bowl.
3. Cover one to two sheet pans with aluminum foil.
4. In a large saucepan, combine sugar, rum, butter, vanilla, and salt.
5. Heat over medium heat, stirring very often.
6. Continue to cook until sugar melts and caramel becomes a pretty brown (caramel) color.
7. Keep stirring as it gets dry before it melts, about 15-20 minutes.
8. Once it melts and turns a dark caramel color, act fast because it scortches quickly.
9. Add the baking soda and keep stirring.
10. Be careful as it bubbles up quickly and almost doubles in quantity.
11. Quickly remove from heat, pour over the popcorn and stir quickly to coat all the corn.
12. Spread the caramel corn out on foil lined sheet pans and allow to cool at least ten minutes.
13. Serve and enjoy!

Kahlua and Espresso Bean Caramel Corn

Ingredients:

2 pkgs. microwave popcorn
1 cup chocolate covered espresso beans
3 cups of granulated white sugar
1/4 cup Kahlua
3 Tbsp unsalted butter
1 Tbsp pure vanilla extract
1.5 tsp salt
1.5 tsp baking soda

Directions:

1. Pop popcorn in microwave according to directions.
2. Place popcorn in a large bowl or foil roasting pan.
3. Sprinkle chocolate covered espresso beans over the popcorn.
4. Cover one to two sheet pans with aluminum foil.
5. In a large saucepan, combine sugar, Kahlua, butter, vanilla, and salt.
6. Heat over medium heat, stirring very often (I stirred nearly continuously).
7. Continue to cook until sugar melts and caramel becomes a pretty brown (caramel) color, about 15-20 minutes.
8. Once it melts and turns a dark caramel color, act fast because it scorches quickly.
9. Add the baking soda (I measured it first and put it in a little bowl so I could add it all at once) and keep stirring.
10. Be careful as it bubbles up quickly and almost doubles in quantity. Quickly remove from heat, pour over the popcorn and espresso beans and stir quickly to coat all the corn.
11. Spread the caramel corn out on foil lined sheet pans and allow to cool at least ten minutes before eating.
12. Add more chocolate covered espresso beans if desired.
13. Serve and enjoy!

Biscoff Popcorn

Ingredients:

2 pkgs. microwave popcorn
16 ounces White Chocolate Candy Coating
1/2 cup Biscoff or Cookie Butter Spread
16 Biscoff cookies (half of an 8.8 ounce package), crushed

Directions:

1. Pop popcorn in microwave according to directions.
2. Place popcorn in a large bowl.
3. Remove any unpopped kernels from popped popcorn.
4. Melt white chocolate candy coating as directed on the package.
5. Once melted, stir in Biscoff spread. Mix until well combined.
6. Pour over popped popcorn and stir to coat all the popcorn.
7. Once mostly coated, pour in crushed cookies and continue stirring until everything is coated in white chocolate.
8. Spread out onto a large sheet pan to cool.
9. Break into pieces.
10. Serve and enjoy!

Cranberry Popcorn Snack Mix

Ingredients:

2 pkgs. microwave popcorn
3 tbsps. dried cranberries
3 tbsps. diced dried plums
1 tbsp. chia seeds
2 tbsps. almond slivers, toasted
3 tbsps. dark chocolate M&M candies
3/4 cup of white chocolate chips, melted

Directions:

1. Pop popcorn in microwave according to directions.
2. Line a rimmed sheet pan with parchment paper or silpat mat.
3. Set aside.
4. Mix all ingredients together except white chocolate.
5. Mix melted white chocolate with other ingredients, stirring so that everything is coated.
6. Spread onto prepared pan and let harden.
7. Break into pieces.
8. Serve and enjoy!

White Chocolate Brown Sugar Popcorn

Ingredients:

2 pkgs. microwave popcorn
1 cup white chocolate chips, divided
1/4 cup brown sugar
1 tsp. cinnamon
1 cup mixed nuts

Directions:

1. Pop popcorn in microwave according to directions.
2. Place popcorn in a large mixing bowl.
3. Set aside.
4. Melt 3/4-cup white chocolate chips.
5. Pour melted chocolate chips over popcorn and stir until combined.
6. Add brown sugar and cinnamon and continue to stir until well blended.
7. Mix in the remaining chocolate chips and mixed nuts.
8. Serve and enjoy!

Brownie Cookie Dough Popcorn

Ingredients:

2 pkgs. microwave popcorn
2 cups mini marshmallows
1/2 cup dry brownie mix
5 oz. vanilla CandiQuik
5 oz. chocolate CandiQuik
1/2 cup mini chocolate chips
1 cup cookie dough candy bites
1/4 cup sprinkles

Directions:

1. Pop popcorn in microwave according to directions.
2. Combine the popcorn and marshmallows in a large bowl.
3. Set aside.
4. Place both flavors of CandiQuik in a microwave safe bowl and heat for 30 seconds.
5. Stir and repeat until melted and smooth.
6. Add the dry brownie mix to the melted chocolate and stir until dissolved.
7. Pour over the popcorn. Toss with your hands until everything is coated.
8. Stir in the cookie dough bites and the chocolate chips.
9. Pour the coated popcorn onto a large baking sheet that is covered with parchment paper.
10. Sprinkle the sprinkles over the popcorn before it sets up.
11. Let set before breaking into chunks.
12. Serve and enjoy!

Chocolate Caramel Popcorn

Ingredients:

2 pkgs. microwave popcorn
2 cups coarsely chopped mixed nuts (optional)
1 package (8 ounces) semi-sweet chocolate squares
1 cup packed brown sugar
½ cup Karo® Corn Syrup
½ cup butter
½ tsp. baking soda

Directions:

1. Pop popcorn in microwave according to directions.
2. Preheat oven to 225 degrees F. Spray a 15 x 10-inch baking pan with cooking spray.
3. Combine popcorn and nuts in baking pan and place in oven to keep warm.
4. Heat chocolate, brown sugar, corn syrup and butter in a 2-quart saucepan over medium heat until boiling, stirring occasionally
5. Boil 5 minutes, stirring constantly.
6. Remove from heat and immediately stir in baking soda.
7. Pour chocolate-caramel mixture carefully over popcorn and nuts.
8. Use cooking spray-coated tongs or a spatula to toss the popcorn and chocolate-caramel mixture.
9. Bake popcorn for 60 minutes stirring popcorn about halfway through.
10. Let popcorn cool completely on wire rack.
11. Break popcorn into bite-sized pieces.
12. Serve and enjoy!

Butter Pecan Cake Kettle Corn Popcorn

Ingredients:

2 pkgs. microwave popcorn
1 tbsp. vegetable oil
1 tbsp. butter
1/4 cup popcorn kernels
3 tbsps. sugar
1/2 tsp. salt
4 sections (8 ounces) white candy melts
1/2 cup butter pecan cake mix
1 cup toasted pecans (toast in a frying pan over low heat, stirring often, just until you smell them)

Directions:

1. Pop popcorn in microwave according to directions.
2. Sprinkle with salt and add to a large bowl.
3. Melt candy melts. Stir in cake mix. Pour over popcorn.
4. Add toasted pecans and stir until all the candy is incorporated.
5. Turn out onto a baking sheet covered with wax paper and chill until candy hardens.
6. Serve and enjoy!

Spiced Chocolate Popcorn

Ingredients:

2 pkgs. microwave popcorn
2 tsp. chili powder
1 tsp. cumin
1/2 tsp. salt
pinch of cayenne
2 tbsp. butter, melted
3 ounces dark or semisweet chocolate, melted in the microwave or double boiler

Directions:

1. Pop popcorn in microwave according to directions.
2. Put popcorn in a large bowl.
3. In a small bowl, whisk together the chili powder, cumin, salt and cayenne until combined.
4. When the popcorn is ready, measure out about 4 cups.
5. Then toss the popcorn with the melted butter and the chili mixture until it is evenly coated.
6. Spread the popcorn out in a single layer on a piece of wax paper, or a foil-covered baking sheet.
7. Use a fork or a pastry bag to drizzle the chocolate over the popcorn.
8. Let it rest for 15 minutes for the popcorn to return to room temperature.
9. Transfer to a bowl.
10. Serve and enjoy!

White Chocolate Lemon Popcorn

Ingredients:

2 pkgs. microwave popcorn
12 oz. white candy melts
2 1/2 Tbsp lemon zest
2 Tbsp fresh lemon juice

Directions:

1. Pop popcorn in microwave according to directions.
2. Put popcorn in a large bowl.
3. Melt white candy melts in a microwave safe bowl, on 50% power, in 30 second intervals, stirring after each interval until melted and smooth.
4. Pour melted white candy melts over popcorn and toss with a rubber spatula until evenly coated.
5. Sprinkle lemon zest over popcorn and toss until evenly distributed.
6. Preheat oven to 275 degrees F.
7. Allow coated popcorn to dry at room temperature, about 10-15 minutes, then drizzle lemon juice over popcorn and toss well to evenly coat.
8. Spread popcorn onto a rimmed cookie sheet and bake in preheated oven for 15 - 20 minutes until lightly golden. Allow popcorn to cool completely, store in an airtight container or large ziploc bag (note: this is best enjoyed the day it's made or one day following).
9. Serve and enjoy!

Chocolate Crispies Popcorn

Ingredients:

2 pkgs. microwave popcorn
2/3 cup brown sugar, packed
2/3 cup light corn syrup
3 Tbsp butter
1 tsp salt
1/2 cup creamy peanut butter
2 cups crispy rice cereal
1 cup semisweet chocolate chips

Directions:

1. Pop popcorn in microwave according to directions.
2. Put popcorn in a large bowl.
3. Preheat oven to 250 degrees F.
4. Line a large jelly roll or roasting pan with parchment paper.
5. In a medium sauce pan combine brown sugar, corn syrup, butter and salt.
6. Bring to a boil and let boil on medium heat for 3 minutes.
7. Remove from heat and stir in peanut butter until smooth.

8. Pour peanut butter caramel over top the popcorn and before mixing sprinkle the cereal on top.
9. Mix everything together, making sure the popcorn and cereal get coated in mixture.
10. Spread popcorn into the prepared pan and bake for 1 hour, stirring every 15 minutes.
11. When popcorn is done spread it out onto a parchment lined counter to cool, breaking apart large pieces.
12. Sprinkle chopped candy bars evenly over top.
13. Melt chocolate chips in a heavy zip-top container in 30 second increments, squeezing after each, until melted. Snip off the end of the bag and drizzle over top popcorn and candy bars.
14. Allow chocolate to set completely.
15. Serve and enjoy!

Peanut Butter and Jelly Popcorn

Ingredients:

2 pkgs. microwave popcorn
1 cup white chocolate, divided
1 1/2 tbsp. Welch's Natural Grape Jelly Spread
1 tbsp. peanut butter

Directions:

1. Pop popcorn in microwave according to directions.
2. Divide Popcorn into two separate bowls.
3. Over medium low heat on the stove top, melt 1/2 cup white chocolate with 1 tbsp. peanut butter. Stir until smooth. Pour over 1 bowl of the popcorn. Use a rubber spatula to mix well and coat thoroughly. Spread out on a silicon mat or parchment paper to let cool.
4. Meanwhile, melt the remaining 1/2 cup white chocolate with 1 1/2 tbsp grape jelly over medium low heat on the stove top. Stir until smooth. Pour over the other bowl of popcorn, and stir with rubber spatula to coat well. Spread out on silicon mat or parchment paper to let cool.
5. Once both batches of popcorn are cooled enough that the coatings are set, mix them both together in a bowl and serve!
6. Serve and enjoy!

Bourbon Toffee Popcorn

Ingredients:

2 pkgs. microwave popcorn
1 tsp salt
1 cup sugar
1/4 cup water
1 tbsp. butter, room temperature
1/2 tsp vanilla bean paste
1 tbsp. bourbon

Directions:

1. Pop popcorn in microwave according to directions.
2. Toss the popcorn with salt.
3. Preheat the oven to 350 degrees.
4. Mix the sugar and water in a medium sauce pan and bring the mixture to a boil.
5. Let the sugar and water cook, boiling over medium heat, about 10-15 minutes, until the sugar is starting to caramelize and is turning a golden / amber color.
6. Lower the heat to low and stir in the butter.
7. Let the mixture cook for another minute, then remove the pan from heat.
8. Stir in the vanilla and bourbon.
9. Pour the toffee over the popcorn and toss everything together.
10. Lay the toffee popcorn out in a single layer on a parchment-lined baking sheet, and bake for 10 minutes at 350.
11. Remove from the oven and let the toffee set before breaking up and serving.
12. Serve and enjoy!

Chocolate Caramel Popcorn

Ingredients:

2 pkgs. microwave popcorn
1 cup butter
2 cups light brown sugar
1/2 cup light corn syrup
1 tsp. salt
1/2 tsp. baking soda
1 tsp. vanilla extract
20 "fun size" Twix candy bars, chopped
2 cups semi-sweet chocolate chips, melted-to drizzle over popcorn

Directions:

1. Pop popcorn in microwave according to directions.
2. Preheat oven to 250 degrees F.
3. Place popcorn in a large bowl and set aside.
4. In a medium saucepan over medium heat, melt butter.
5. Stir in brown sugar, corn syrup, and salt.
6. Bring to a boil, stirring constantly.
7. Boil without stirring for 4 minutes.
8. Remove from heat and stir in baking soda and vanilla extract. Pour caramel in a thin stream over popcorn, stirring to coat.
9. Gently stir until all of the popcorn is covered.
10. Place popcorn on two large shallow baking sheets and bake in preheated oven, stirring every 15 minutes, for about an hour.
11. Remove popcorn from oven and let cool completely.
12. Break popcorn into pieces and mix in chopped Twix candy bars.
13. Drizzle popcorn with melted chocolate. Let the popcorn sit until chocolate hardens, about 30 minutes. Store at room temperature in an airtight container.
14. Serve and enjoy!

Pumpkin Pie Spice Popcorn

Ingredients:

2 pkgs. microwave popcorn
1/3 cup Olive Oil
1 tbsp. Pumpkin Pie Spice
2 tbsps. granulated sugar
1/4-1/2 tsp. Kosher salt, divided

Directions:

1. Pop popcorn in microwave according to directions.
2. Preheat oven to 325 degrees F.
3. Place popcorn on a parchment paper lined baking sheet in a single layer.
4. In a small bowl, blend together olive oil, pumpkin pie spice, sugar and ¼ tsp. kosher salt.
5. Once blended, drizzle over popcorn until evenly dispersed.
6. Stir the popcorn around on the baking sheet until popcorn is coated.
7. Bake for 8-10 minutes, stopping to stir at the 5 minute mark.
8. Remove from the oven'
9. Sprinkle with salt.
10. Serve and enjoy!

Chocolate Chip Cookie Popcorn

Ingredients:

2 pkgs. microwave popcorn
1/2 (16.5 oz.) pkgs. of Chocolate Chip refrigerated cookie dough
16 oz white vanilla almond bark
1/2 cup mini chocolate chips

Directions:

1. Pop popcorn in microwave according to directions.
2. Make 8 cookies from the cookie dough, according to the package directions.
3. Cool completely, then lightly crumble.
4. Lay out a piece of waxed paper.
5. Put popcorn in a large bowl.
6. Place the vanilla almond bark in a microwave safe bowl and melt according to the package directions.
7. Pour over the popcorn.
8. Add in the crumbled cookies and the mini chocolate chips. Stir gently to combine.
9. Pour the popcorn onto the prepared waxed paper.
10. Let cool until the bark sets up, about 20 minutes.
11. Serve and enjoy!

Toasted Coconut Popcorn

Ingredients:

2 pkgs. microwave popcorn
1/2 cup butter
1/4 cup sugar
1/4 tsp. coconut extract
1 1/2 cups shredded coconut

Directions:

1. Pop popcorn in microwave according to directions.
2. In a small saucepan, melt butter. Add sugar, and stir to dissolve.
3. Bring to a boil, and let boil 1-2 minutes.
4. Remove from heat and add coconut extract.
5. Place coconut on a baking sheet, and bake at 400 degrees F for 5-10 minutes until lightly toasted.
6. Stir, and bake another 2-3 minutes.
7. Place popcorn and coconut in a large bowl.
8. Pour butter mixture over the top, and stir to coat.
9. Serve and enjoy!

Kettle Corn Mix Popcorn

Ingredients:

1/2 cup confectioners' sugar
2 tbsps. granulated sugar
1 tsp. kosher salt
1/4 cup vegetable oil
3/4 cup popcorn kernels

Directions:

1. Mix confectioners' sugar, granulated sugar and kosher salt in a small bowl.
2. Set aside.
3. Heat a few popcorn kernels in vegetable oil in a large pot over medium-high heat until one pops.
4. Add popcorn kernels and cover.
5. Cook, shaking the pot occasionally, until the popcorn starts rapidly popping.
6. Crack the lid open and pour in the sugar mixture.
7. Cover and cook, shaking the pot, until the popping subsides.
8. Serve and enjoy!

Savoury Popcorn Recipes

Cheesy Popcorn

Ingredients:

1 bag microwave popcorn
1/4 cup grated cheddar cheese
6 tbsp. butter

Directions:

1. Pop popcorn in microwave according to package directions.
2. Pick out any un-popped kernels.
3. Pour into a large bowl.
4. Sprinkle grated cheese over top.
5. Melt the butter.
6. Drizzle melted butter on top of cheese.
7. Toss to coat well.
8. Serve and enjoy!

Bacon Popcorn

Ingredients:

2 pkgs. microwave popcorn
6 slices bacon (maple flavored or plain)
1 tsp. salt

Directions:

1. Pop popcorn in microwave according to directions.
2. Cook the bacon until crisp.
3. Remove the bacon and allow it to cool on a paper towel, reserving the drippings.
4. Pour the popcorn in a bowl.
5. Pick out any un-popped kernels.
6. Pour the bacon drippings over the popcorn and mix to combine.
7. Crumble the bacon and mix with the popcorn.
8. Serve and enjoy!

Coconut Curry Popcorn

Ingredients:

2 bags of microwave popcorn
1 tbsp. coconut oil
2 tbsps. toasted coconut flakes
1 tbsp. curry powder
2 tsps. ginger powder

Directions:

1. Pop popcorn in microwave according to directions.
2. Pick out any un-popped kernels.
3. Put popcorn in a large bowl.
4. Melt coconut oil and drizzle on top of warm popcorn.
5. Sprinkle coconut flakes, curry powder, and ginger on top.
6. Cover with lid and shake vigorously for 10-15 seconds.
7. Serve and enjoy!

Ketchup Popcorn

Ingredients:

2 bags of microwave popcorn
3 tbsps. ketchup
2 tbsps. butter
1 tbsps. granulated sugar
8 cups plain popcorn
salt

Directions:

1. Pop popcorn in microwave according to directions.
2. Pour popcorn on to a baking sheet.
3. Pick out any un-popped kernels.
4. Mix ketchup with butter and granulated sugar in a small saucepan set on medium heat.
5. Whisk until sugar dissolves.
6. Drizzle over popcorn.
7. Mix until coated.
8. Sprinkle with salt.
9. Bake at 300 degrees for 12 to 15 minutes, stirring occasionally, until popcorn is dry and crisp.
10. Serve and enjoy!

Pizza Popcorn

Ingredients:

2 bags of plain microwave popcorn
1/3 cup butter
1/4 cup Parmesan cheese
1/2 tsp. garlic powder
1/2 tsp. dried oregano
1/2 tsp. dried basil
1/2 tsp. onion powder
1/4 tsp. salt

Directions:

1. Pop popcorn in microwave according to directions.
2. Pour popcorn in an ungreased 13"x9"2-inch baking pan.
3. Pick out any un-popped kernels.
4. Melt butter in a small saucepan.
5. Add the remaining ingredients to the butter.
6. Pour the mixture over the popcorn and mix well.
7. Bake uncovered at 350 degrees for 15 minutes.
8. Serve and enjoy!

Taco Popcorn

Ingredients:

2 pkgs. microwave popcorn
1/4 cup butter
1 tbsp. taco seasoning
Salt to taste

Directions:

1. Pop popcorn in microwave according to directions.
2. Pick out any un-popped kernels.
3. Melt butter.
4. Mix in taco seasoning.
5. Toss butter mixture with popped popcorn in a large bowl.
6. Salt to taste.
7. Serve and enjoy!

Sour Cream and Onion Popcorn

Ingredients:

2 bags microwave popcorn
2 tbsps. extra virgin olive oil
3 tbsps. fresh dill, chopped
3 tbsps. grated Parmesan cheese
3 tbsps. powdered buttermilk
1 1/2 tbsps. onion powder
1 tsp. garlic powder
1 tsp. sea salt
1/2 tsp. ground pepper

Directions:

1. Pop popcorn in microwave according to directions.
2. Pour into a large bowl.
3. Pick out any un-popped kernels.
4. Drizzle the popcorn with olive oil
5. Toss well to coat.
6. In small bowl, whisk together dill, cheese, buttermilk, onion powder, garlic powder, salt and pepper.
7. Pour it over the popcorn.
8. Toss the popcorn to coat it in the mixture.
9. Serve and enjoy!

Doritos Popcorn

3 pkgs. microwave popcorn
1/4 cup nutritional yeast
2 tsps. salt
1 tsp. ground cumin
1 tsp. garlic powder
1 tsp. onion powder
1 tsp. paprika
1 tsp. chili powder
1/8 tsp. cayenne pepper

Directions:

1. Pop popcorn in microwave according to directions.
2. Combine nutritional yeast, salt, cumin, garlic powder, onion powder, paprika, chili powder, and cayenne pepper in a small bowl.
3. Place popcorn in a bowl.
4. Add nutritional yeast mixture and toss to coat.
5. Serve and enjoy!

Popcorn Nachos

Ingredients:

2 pkgs. microwave popcorn
1/2 cup butter, melted
1 tsp. crushed red pepper
1 tsp. ground cumin
1 tsp. paprika
1/2 cup shredded Cheddar cheese

Directions:

1. Pop popcorn in microwave according to directions.
2. In a small bowl, mix together butter, crushed red pepper, cumin and paprika.
3. Place popcorn in a large bowl.
4. Sprinkle with the butter mixture and Cheddar cheese.
5. Toss until well mixed.
6. Serve and enjoy!

Lemon Butter Popcorn

Ingredients:

2 pkgs. microwave popcorn
6 tbsps. butter
1 1/2 tsps. grated lemon zest
Toss with 2 tsps. kosher salt

Directions:

1. Pop popcorn in microwave according to directions.
2. Cook butter in a skillet over medium heat until browned, about 7 minutes.
3. Remove from the heat and stir in lemon zest.
4. Drizzle over popcorn.
5. Toss with kosher salt.
6. Serve and enjoy!

Ranch Popcorn

Ingredients:

2 pkgs. microwave popcorn
4 tbsps. butter
1 (1 ounce) packet ranch seasoning mix
2 tbsps. chopped chives
Salt to taste

Directions:

1. Pop popcorn in microwave according to directions.
2. Melt butter with ranch seasoning mix.
3. Toss with popcorn and chives.
4. Season with salt.
5. Serve and enjoy!

Garlic Herb Popcorn

Ingredients:

2 pkgs. microwave popcorn
4 tbsps. butter
4 grated garlic cloves
1 tsp. fresh rosemary, finely chopped
1 tsp. sage
1 tsp. thyme
2 tsps. Kosher salt

Directions:

1. Pop popcorn in microwave according to directions.
2. Melt butter in a saucepan.
3. Add garlic cloves, rosemary, sage and thyme.
4. Cook 1 minute.
5. Drizzle over popcorn.
6. Toss popcorn with kosher salt.
7. Serve and enjoy!

Parmesan Rosemary Popcorn

Ingredients:

2 pkgs. microwave popcorn
1/2 cup grated parmesan
3 tbsps. olive oil
1 tbsp. fresh rosemary, finely chopped
2 tsps. Kosher salt

Directions:

1. Pop popcorn in microwave according to directions.
2. Pour popcorn in a large bowl.
3. Toss remaining ingredients over hot popcorn.
4. Serve and enjoy!

Frito Popcorn

Ingredients:

2 pkgs. microwave popcorn
6 tbsps. melted butter
4 cups Fritos
2 tbsps. chili powder
2 cups shredded cheddar cheese
2 chopped scallions
Salt to taste

Directions:

5. Pop popcorn in microwave according to directions.
6. Toss popcorn, butter, Fritos and chili powder together.
7. Spread on a baking sheet.
8. Top with cheddar cheese and scallions.
9. Bake at 350 degrees F until the cheese melts, about 3 minutes.
10. Season with salt to taste.
11. Serve and enjoy!

Truffle Popcorn

Ingredients:

2 pkgs. microwave popcorn
6 tbsps. melted butter
1 1/2 tbsps. truffle oil
1/4 cup grated parmesan
1 tsp. kosher salt
1/2 tsp. pepper.

Directions:

1. Pop popcorn in microwave according to directions.
2. Pour popcorn in a large bowl.
3. Toss remaining ingredients over hot popcorn.
4. Serve and enjoy!

Veggie Delight Popcorn

Ingredients:

2 pkgs. microwave popcorn
4 cups each mixed veggie chips, divided
4 cups dehydrated snap peas, divided
Salt to taste

Directions:

5. Pop popcorn in microwave according to directions.
6. Pulse 2 cups veggie chips with 2 cups snap peas in a food processor until powdery.
7. Toss with popcorn, 2 cups veggie chips and 2 cups dehydrated snap peas.
8. Season with salt to taste.
9. Serve and enjoy!

Crunchy Ramen Popcorn

Ingredients:

2 pkgs. microwave popcorn
2 (3 ounce) packages ramen noodles (any flavor), flavor packets reserved
Vegetable oil for frying

Directions:

1. Pop popcorn in microwave according to directions.
2. Soak ramen noodles in warm water, 4 minutes.
3. Pull apart the noodles and pat dry.
4. Heat 1/4 inch vegetable oil in a large skillet over medium-high heat.
5. Fry the noodles in a single layer until crisp.
6. Drain.
7. Break into pieces.
8. Toss noodles with popcorn, and the flavor packets to taste.
9. Serve and enjoy!

Three-Cheese Popcorn

Ingredients:

2 pkgs. microwave popcorn
2 cups shredded cheddar,
1 cup grated parmesan cheese
1/2 cup grated pecorino cheese
Salt to taste

Directions:

1. Pop popcorn in microwave according to directions.
2. Toss popcorn with cheddar, parmesan and pecorino cheese.
3. Spread on baking sheets.
4. Bake at 350 degrees F until the cheddar melts, about 3 minutes.
5. Season with salt to taste.
6. Serve and enjoy!

Gourmet Mushroom Cheese Popcorn

Ingredients:

2 pkgs. microwave popcorn
1/2 cup porcini mushrooms, dried
2 tbsps. fresh parsley, chopped
1 1/2 tsps. kosher salt
6 tbsps. butter, melted
1 cup gruyere cheese, finely grated

Directions:

1. Pop popcorn in microwave according to directions.
2. Pulse mushrooms in a spice grinder until powdery.
3. Add parsley and salt and pulse again until powdery.
4. Drizzle melted butter over popcorn.
5. Toss with the porcini powder and gruyere.
6. Serve and enjoy!

Everything Bagel Popcorn

Ingredients:

2 pkgs. microwave popcorn
4 cups bagel chips, broken
6 tbsps. melted butter
2 tbsps. each white sesame seeds
2 tbsps. each black sesame seeds
1 tbsp. each caraway seeds
Granulated onion to taste
Granulated garlic to taste
1 1/2 tsps. kosher salt

Directions:

1. Pop popcorn in microwave according to directions.
2. Toss all ingredients together with hot popcorn and enjoy!
3. Serve and enjoy!

Bacon Chive Popcorn

Ingredients:

2 pkgs. microwave popcorn
6 slices bacon
2 tbsps. butter, melted
1/2 cup chopped chives
1/2 tsp. cayenne
Salt to taste

Directions:

1. Pop popcorn in microwave according to directions.
2. Cook bacon until crisp.
3. Drain on paper towels, reserving the drippings.
4. Crumble the bacon.
5. Drizzle 2 tbsps. of the reserved bacon drippings and the melted butter over the popcorn.
6. Toss with the bacon, chives and cayenne.
7. Salt to taste.
8. Serve and enjoy!

Movie Theater Popcorn

Ingredients:

Coconut oil
Popcorn kernels
Real butter, melted
Salt or movie popcorn seasoning

Directions:

1. In a heavy bottom sauce pan add enough coconut oil to cover the bottom of the pan.
2. Turn the heat on to medium-high.
3. Add one or two kernels to the pan.
4. Cover.
5. When you hear the one kernel pop, add the rest of the kernels (up to enough to cover the bottom of the pan).
6. Stir.
7. Put a lid on the pan and shake carefully.
8. When the rest of the kernels start popping, turn the heat down.
9. Shake the pan carefully every now and then to avoid burning.
10. When the corn slows down popping, remove from heat and let it finish popping.
11. Salt and butter if desired.
12. Serve and enjoy!

Vanilla Popcorn

Ingredients:

3/4 cup unpopped popcorn
1/4 cup corn oil
1 (4 inch) vanilla bean, split lengthwise
1 tbsp. superfine sugar
Salt to taste
2 tbsps. butter, melted

Directions:

1. Heat corn oil in a large pot over medium-high or high heat for a minute.
2. Add one kernel of popcorn to the oil.
3. When the kernel pops, pour in the remaining popcorn and the vanilla bean.
4. Place a lid on the pot, and shake gently until the corn starts to pop. Shake vigorously until the popping subsides.
5. Remove from the heat, and pour into a large bowl.
6. Remove the vanilla bean from the corn.
7. Scrape seeds from the vanilla bean, and mix with sugar.
8. Stir sugar, salt and melted butter into the corn until evenly coated.
9. Serve and enjoy!

Dill Pickle Popcorn

Ingredients:

2 bags microwave popcorn
1 tbsp. coriander seed
1 tbsp. kosher salt
1-1/2 tsps. dill weed
1/2 tsp. mustard seed
1/2 tsp. garlic powder
1/2 tsp. onion powder
1/2 tsp. celery seed
1/2 tsp. citric acid
1/2 cup butter, melted

Directions:

1. Pop popcorn in microwave according to package directions.
2. Place all other ingredients except butter in a spice grinder and process until smooth.
3. Set aside.
4. Drizzle popcorn with melted butter.
5. Start sprinkling with dill pickle flavoring and tasting until desired flavor is reached.
6. Serve and enjoy!

Spicy Popcorn Recipes

Wasabi Soy Sauce Popcorn

Ingredients:

2 bags of microwave popcorn
3 tbsps. coconut oil or butter
1 tbsp. soy sauce
2 tsps. wasabi powder
1 tsp. sea salt
1 tsp. red pepper flakes

Directions:

1. Pop popcorn in microwave according to directions.
2. Pick out any un-popped kernels.
3. Melt the coconut oil or butter in microwave.
4. Add in soy sauce and wasabi powder and stir until completely mixed.
5. Pour the oil or butter mixture over warm popcorn and mix until coated.
6. Sprinkle on the sea salt and red pepper flakes.
7. Mix again.
8. Serve and enjoy!

Mustard Pretzel Popcorn

Ingredients:

2 pkgs. microwave popcorn
4 cups mini pretzels
4 tbsps. melted butter
2 tbsps. dijon mustard
1 tsp. sugar
1/2 tsp. kosher salt

Directions:

1. Pop popcorn in microwave according to directions.
2. Whisk together melted butter with dijon mustard, sugar and salt.
3. Drizzle over popcorn and toss with the mini pretzels.
4. Serve and enjoy!

Jamaican Jerk Popcorn

Ingredients:

2 pkgs. microwave popcorn
5 tbsps. butter, melted
1 1/2 tbsps. jerk seasoning
1 tsp. curry powder
1/4 tsp. cayenne
1 cup toasted coconut
2 tsps. grated lime zest
Salt to taste

Directions:

1. Pop popcorn in microwave according to directions.
2. Whisk together butter, jerk seasoning, curry powder and cayenne.
3. Drizzle over popcorn.
4. Toss popcorn with coconut and grated lime zest.
5. Season with salt.
6. Serve and enjoy!

Za'atar Popcorn

Ingredients:

2 pkgs. microwave popcorn

6 tbsps. melted butter

2 tbsps. za'atar spice blend

1 tsp. kosher salt

4 cups broken pita chips

Directions:

1. Pop popcorn in microwave according to directions.
2. In a small bowl, whisk together butter, za'atar spice blend and kosher salt.
3. Drizzle over popcorn.
4. toss with 4 cups broken pita chips.
5. Serve and enjoy!

Mole Popcorn

Ingredients:

2 pkgs. microwave popcorn
6 tbsps. jarred mole sauce
6 tbsps. melted butter
salt to taste

Directions:

1. Pop popcorn in microwave according to directions.
2. In a small bowl, whisk together butter and jarred mole sauce.
3. Toss with popcorn.
4. Season with salt.
5. Serve and enjoy!

Cajun Popcorn

Ingredients:

2 pkgs. microwave popcorn
4 tbsps. butter, melted
1 tbsp. Cajun seasoning
1 tsp. grated lemon zest
1/4 tsp. cayenne and
2 scallions, chopped
Salt to taste

Directions:

1. Pop popcorn in microwave according to directions.
2. Melt butter with Cajun seasoning, grated lemon zest, cayenne and scallions.
3. Drizzle over popcorn and toss.
4. Season with salt.
5. Serve and enjoy!

Barbecue Popcorn

Ingredients:

2 pkgs. microwave popcorn
4 tbsps. butter
1 tsp. cumin
1 tsp. paprika
1 tsp. granulated garlic
1 tsp. chili powder
1 tsp. barbecue sauce
Pinch of cayenne
4 cups barbecue potato chips, lightly crushed
Salt to taste

Directions:

1. Pop popcorn in microwave according to directions.
2. Melt butter with cumin, paprika, garlic, chili powder, barbecue sauce, and cayenne.
3. Toss with popcorn and barbecue potato chips.
4. Season with salt.
5. Serve and enjoy!

Bacon Jalapeno Popcorn

Ingredients:

2 pkgs. microwave popcorn
6 slices bacon
2 tbsps. butter, melted
1/2 cup chopped chives
Salt to taste
4 jalapenos, thinly sliced
1/2 cup cornstarch
1/3 cup seltzer
Vegetable oil for frying if needed

Directions:

1. Pop popcorn in microwave according to directions.
2. Cook bacon until crisp.
3. Transfer bacon to paper towels, reserving 2 tbsps. of the drippings.
4. Crumble the bacon.
5. Whisk seltzer with the corn starch.
6. Dip the jalapenos in the corn starch / seltzer mixture and then fry the jalapenos in the drippings or vegetable oil until golden and crisp, 2 minutes.
7. Drain on paper towels.
8. Drizzle 2 tbsps. of the reserved bacon drippings and the melted butter over the popcorn.
9. Toss the popcorn with the fried jalapenos and bacon.
10. Salt to taste.
11. Serve and enjoy!

Spicy Pork Rind Popcorn

Ingredients:

2 pkgs. microwave popcorn
1/4 cup vegetable oil
1 1/2 tbsps. chili powder
2 tsps. grated lime zest
1/2 tsp. cayenne
2 cups pork rinds
1 tbsp. lime juice
Salt to taste

Directions:

1. Pop popcorn in microwave according to directions.
2. Heat vegetable oil with chili powder, lime zest and cayenne in a skillet over medium heat for 2 minutes.
3. Drizzle over popcorn.
4. Toss with pork rinds and lime juice.
5. Salt to taste.
6. Serve and enjoy!

Tex Mex Popcorn

Ingredients:

2 pkgs. microwave popcorn
1/2 tsp. salt
1/2 tsp. garlic powder
1/2 tsp. ground cumin
1 tsp. ancho chile powder
2 tbsps. melted butter
1/2 cup sun dried tomatoes, diced (dried vacuum sealed, not in oil)
3/4 cup cooked chorizo, crumbled
3/4 cup queso fresco, crumbled
1 firm but ripe avocado, diced

Directions:

1. Pop popcorn in microwave according to package directions.
2. Mix the salt and spices together in a small bowl.
3. Pour popcorn in a large bowl.
4. Drizzle popcorn with butter.
5. Sprinkle spice blend over popcorn and toss.
6. Shake until thoroughly coated, then
7. Toss with sun dried tomatoes.
8. Put popcorn into smaller serving bowls and top each bowl with crumbled chorizo, queso fresco, and diced avocado.
9. Serve and enjoy!

Szechuan Popcorn

Ingredients:

2 pkgs. microwave popcorn
1 cup peanuts
1 cup dried arbol chiles
1/2 cup peanut oil
1/2 cup sesame seeds
1/2 cup Szechuan peppercorns
4 tsps. sugar
4 tsps. kosher salt
2 tbsps. toasted sesame oil

Directions:

1. Pop popcorn in microwave according to directions.
2. Heat peanuts, chiles, peanut oil, sesame seeds, Szechuan peppercorns, sugar and salt in a large skillet over medium heat until the nuts and chiles are toasted, 4 minutes.
3. Pour over popcorn.
4. Toss with sesame oil.
5. Serve and enjoy!

Sriracha Lime Popcorn

Ingredients:

2 pkgs. microwave popcorn
5 tbsps. butter, melted
1/4 cup Sriracha sauce
1 1/2 tsps. grated lime zest
1 tbsp. lime juice
Salt to taste

Directions:

1. Pop popcorn in microwave according to directions.
2. Whisk melted butter with Sriracha sauce, lime zest and lime juice.

3. Drizzle over popcorn and toss.
4. Season with salt to taste.
5. Serve and enjoy!

Chipotle Popcorn

Ingredients:

2 pkgs. microwave popcorn
4 tbsps. butter
2 tbsps. chipotle hot sauce
1 tbsp. chipotle chile powder
2 cups corn nuts
Salt to taste

Directions:

1. Pop popcorn in microwave according to directions.
2. Melt butter with chipotle hot sauce and chipotle chile powder.
3. Drizzle over popcorn.
4. Toss with corn nuts.
5. Season with salt.
6. Serve and enjoy!

Spicy Sesame Popcorn

Ingredients:

2 pkgs. microwave popcorn
6 tbsps. butter
2/3 cup sesame seeds
1 tbsp. sugar
1 tbsp. kosher salt

Directions:

1. Pop popcorn in microwave according to directions.
2. In a small skillet, heat butter and sesame seeds over medium heat until the seeds are toasted, about 5 minutes.
3. Stir in sugar and salt.
4. Toss with popcorn.
5. Serve and enjoy!

Sushi Popcorn

Ingredients:

2 pkgs. microwave popcorn
1 1/2 tbsps. vegetable oil
1 1/2 tbsps. soy sauce
2 tsps. toasted sesame oil
2 tsps. rice vinegar
2 cups roasted seaweed snacks, torn
1 cup wasabi peas

Directions:

1. Pop popcorn in microwave according to directions.
2. Whisk vegetable oil and soy sauce with toasted sesame oil and rice vinegar.
3. Drizzle over popcorn.
4. Toss with seaweed snacks and wasabi peas.
5. Serve and enjoy!

Buffalo Wings Popcorn

Ingredients:

3 bags of microwave popcorn
1 tsp. Granulated Garlic
1/2 tsp. Dill
1/4 tsp. Cumin
1/2 tsp. Sea Salt
4 tbsps. Butter
2 tsps. hot sauce

Directions:

1. Pop popcorn in microwave according to directions.
2. Pick out any un-popped kernels.
3. In a small bowl combine granulated garlic, dill, cumin, and sea salt.
4. Set aside.
5. Melt the butter.
6. Add the sauce.
7. Mix well.
8. Toss butter with popcorn in a large bowl.
9. Toss with seasoning.
10. Serve and enjoy!

Chili Popcorn

Ingredients:

2 bags of microwave popcorn
1/2 tbsp. margarine
1/2 tsp. popcorn salt
1/8 tsp. garlic powder
1 1/4 tsps. chili powder
1/4 tsp. ground cumin

Directions:

1. Pop popcorn in microwave according to directions.
2. Pour popcorn into a large bowl.
3. Pick out any un-popped kernels.
4. Melt the margarine.
5. Pour the margarine over the popcorn.
6. Stir to coat.
7. Sprinkle popcorn with popcorn salt, garlic powder, chili pepper and cumin.
8. Toss to coat evenly.
9. Serve and enjoy!

Jalapeno Popcorn

Ingredients:

2 pkgs. microwave popcorn
1/4 cup vegetable oil, divided
6 slices pickled jalapeno peppers, drained, or more to taste
1/4 cup butter, melted
1 (1 ounce) package ranch dressing mix

Directions:

1. Pop popcorn in microwave according to directions.
2. Heat 2 tbsps. oil in a small skillet over medium-high heat.
3. Add sliced jalapenos.
4. Cook and stir until browned and crispy, 3 to 5 minutes.
5. Transfer to a small plate with a slotted spoon.
6. Pour melted butter evenly over popcorn.
7. Lightly sprinkle ranch dressing mix over popcorn.
8. Mix to combine.
9. Crumble jalapeno slices and mix in.
10. Serve and enjoy!

Curry Popcorn

2 pkgs. microwave popcorn
1 stick butter
2 cups golden raisins
2 cups pistachios
3 tbsps. sugar
1 tbsp. curry powder
2 tsps. kosher salt

Directions:

1. Pop popcorn in microwave according to directions.
2. Melt butter in a saucepan over low heat.
3. Add raisins, pistachios, sugar and curry powder and cook about 2 minutes.
4. Toss with popcorn and salt.
5. Serve and enjoy!

Thai Curry Popcorn

Ingredients:

2 pkgs. microwave popcorn
4 oz. rice vermicelli
1/4 cup red Thai curry paste
1/4 cup vegetable oil
1 tsp. kosher salt
2 cups roasted cashews

Directions:

1. Pop popcorn in microwave according to directions.
2. Heat vegetable oil in a medium saucepan to 350 degrees F.
3. Fry rice vermicelli until crisp, about 20 seconds.
4. Drain.
5. Warm curry paste, vegetable oil and kosher salt in the microwave, 1 minute.
6. Drizzle over popcorn.
7. Toss with 2 cups roasted cashews and the fried noodles.
8. Serve and enjoy!

Red Hots Popcorn

Ingredients:

2 bags of plain microwave popcorn
¼ cup water
½ cup red hot candies

Directions:

1. Pop popcorn in microwave according to directions.
2. Line a baking sheet with parchment paper.
3. Pour popcorn onto the baking sheet.
4. Pick out any un-popped kernels.
5. Preheat the oven to 250 degrees.
6. In a small saucepan, combine the water and red hots.
7. Stir until candy is melted.
8. Spoon over the popcorn
9. Toss until well mixed.
10. Place baking sheet in the oven and bake for about 20 minutes until the popcorn is almost dry, stirring once halfway thorough.
11. Serve and enjoy!

Maryland Crab Cake Popcorn

Ingredients:

2 bags of plain microwave popcorn
2 tbsp. butter
¼ cup olive oil
Old Bay Seasoning
1 tbsp. sugar
1 tbsp. garlic powder

Directions:

1. Pop popcorn in microwave according to directions.
2. Pour popcorn into a large bowl.
3. Pick out any un-popped kernels.
4. Melt butter and pour over the popcorn, stirring to evenly coat.
5. Sprinkle Old Bay, sugar and garlic powder over popcorn while stirring batch, to evenly distribute.
6. Add seasoning while the popcorn is still hot. This helps the seasoning to stick to the popcorn better.
7. Serve and enjoy!

The End

About the Author

Laura Sommers is the Zombie Prepper Mom! Helping you prepare for the Zombie Apocalypse! She is the #1 Best Selling Author of the "Recipes for the Zombie Apocalypse" cookbook series as well as over 60 other recipe books.

She is a loving wife and mother who lives on a small farm in Baltimore County, Maryland and has a passion for all things domestic especially when it comes to saving money. She has a profitable eBay business and is a couponing addict. Follow her tips and tricks to learn how to make delicious meals on a budget, save money or to learn the latest life hack!

Other books by Laura Sommers

- Egg Recipes For People With Backyard Chickens
- Easy to Make Party Dip Recipes: Chips and Dips and Salsa and Whips!
- Super Slimming Vegan Soup Recipes!: Low Calorie Vegetarian Soups to Help You Lose Weight.
- Egg Recipes For People With Backyard Chickens: Quiche, frittatas, breakfast burritos and many more recipes to be used with eggs from your backyard chickens.
- Inexpensive Low Carb Recipes
- Recipes for the Zombie Apocalypse: Cooking Meals with Shelf Stable Foods

May all of your meals be a banquet
with good friends and good food.

Made in the USA
Coppell, TX
10 October 2021

63838176R00057